Menorca

Travel Guide

Your Ultimate Companion for Unforgettable Adventures, Pristine Beaches and Rich Cultural Heritage

Tyler Rivers

Copyright © 2023 by Tyler Rivers

All rights reserved. No part of this book may be reproduced or transmitted in any form or by any means, electronic or mechanical, including photocopying, recording, or by any information storage and retrieval system, without written permission from the author or publisher.

Disclaimer

The pictures featured in this book are for artistic purposes only and do not necessarily represent the actual locations referenced in the text. While every effort has been made to ensure the accuracy of the information contained in this guide, neither the author nor the publisher assumes any responsibility for errors or omissions, or for any consequences arising from the use of the information contained herein.

Table of Content

CHAPTER 1 7

INTRODUCTION 7

Why Visit Menorca 7

How to Use This Guide 9

CHAPTER 2 10

PLANNING YOUR TRIP 10

When to Visit Menorca 10

Duration of Stay 11

Entry Requirements 11

Getting to Menorca 12

Getting Around Menorca 12

Accommodation Options 13

Packing Essentials 13

CHAPTER 3 15

EXPLORING MENORCA 15

Mahon 15

Ciutadella 16

Other Towns and Villages 17

Beaches and Coves 17

Natural Parks and Reserves 18

Outdoor Activities 19

Water Sports and Diving... 19

CHAPTER 4 21

MENORCA'S CUISINE 21

Traditional Dishes... 21

Local Ingredients and Specialties 22

Popular Restaurants and Cafés... 22

CHAPTER 5 24

MENORCA'S FESTIVALS AND EVENTS 24

Sant Joan Festival 24

Fiestas de Sant Antoni 25

Other Cultural and Music Events 26

CHAPTER 6 28

DAY TRIPS AND EXCURSIONS 28

Isla del Rey 28

Cami de Cavalls 29

Boat Trips to Other Islands.. 30

Nature Reserves and Rural Landscapes 30

CHAPTER 7 32

PRACTICAL INFORMATION 32

Health and Safety Tips 32

Money and Currency Exchange 33

Communication and Internet 34

Local Customs and Etiquette 35

Language and Useful Phrases 36

CHAPTER 8 38

MENORCA WITH KIDS 38

Family-Friendly Attractions 38

Outdoor Activities for Kids 39

Child-Friendly Beaches 40

Practical Tips for Traveling with Kids 40

CHAPTER 9 43

MENORCA'S HIDDEN GEMS 43

Off the Beaten Path Destinations 43

Lesser-Known Beaches and Coves 44

Local Secrets and Recommendations 45

CHAPTER 10 47
  CONCLUSION 47
  Final Tips and Recommendations 49

CHAPTER 1

INTRODUCTION

Menorca, a gem of the Mediterranean, is a captivating island nestled in the Balearic archipelago off the coast of Spain. With its pristine beaches, rich history, and stunning natural landscapes, Menorca offers a unique and unforgettable travel experience. Known for its relaxed atmosphere and unspoiled beauty, the island attracts visitors seeking a tranquil and authentic Mediterranean getaway.

Why Visit Menorca

There are countless reasons to visit Menorca. Whether you are a nature enthusiast, a history buff, a beach lover, or simply in search of a peaceful retreat, Menorca has something to offer everyone. The island boasts a remarkable blend of natural beauty and cultural heritage, providing a diverse range of activities and attractions to explore.

Menorca's coastline is a paradise of turquoise waters, hidden coves, and golden sandy beaches. From secluded bays like Cala Macarella and Cala Mitjana to larger stretches of shoreline like Son Bou and Punta Prima, the island offers a myriad of options for sunbathing, swimming, and water sports.

In addition to its stunning beaches, Menorca is home to an abundance of natural wonders. The island's biosphere reserve, declared by UNESCO in 1993, showcases its commitment to preserving the unique ecosystem and biodiversity. Explore the lush landscapes of Parc Natural de s'Albufera des Grau or take a hike along the famous Cami de Cavalls, a coastal path that encircles the island, offering breathtaking views of the rugged cliffs and crystal-clear waters.

Menorca's history is as captivating as its natural beauty. The island has been shaped by the influence of various civilizations throughout the centuries, leaving behind a rich cultural heritage. Explore the ancient Talaiotic sites, such as Naveta d'es Tudons and Torre d'en Galmés, and immerse yourself in the island's fascinating past. The charming towns of Mahon and Ciutadella boast impressive architecture, picturesque squares, and narrow winding streets that invite you to wander and discover hidden gems at every turn.

How to Use This Guide

This travel guide is designed to help you make the most of your visit to Menorca. It provides comprehensive information and insider tips to ensure a smooth and rewarding travel experience. Whether you are a first-time visitor or a seasoned traveler to the island, this guide will serve as your companion in planning and exploring Menorca.

Each chapter is dedicated to a specific aspect of Menorca, providing detailed insights into its attractions, activities, cuisine, festivals, practical information, and more. You will find recommendations for must-visit places, off-the-beaten-path gems, and practical tips to enhance your trip.

Throughout the guide, you will also find maps, suggested itineraries, and useful contact information to assist you in navigating the island and making informed decisions.

So, grab your sunscreen, pack your bags, and get ready to embark on an unforgettable journey through the enchanting island of Menorca. Whether you seek relaxation, adventure, or a cultural immersion, Menorca is waiting to welcome you with its timeless charm and natural splendor. Let this guide be your gateway to unlocking the treasures of Menorca and creating memories that will last a lifetime.

CHAPTER 2

PLANNING YOUR TRIP

When to Visit Menorca

Choosing the right time to visit Menorca can greatly enhance your travel experience. The island enjoys a Mediterranean climate, with warm summers and mild winters. The peak tourist season in Menorca is from June to August when the weather is hot and the beaches are bustling. However, if you prefer a quieter and more affordable trip, consider visiting during the shoulder seasons of spring (April to May) and autumn (September to October).

During the springtime, Menorca bursts into life with colorful flowers and blooming landscapes. The weather is pleasant, with temperatures ranging from 15°C to 23°C (59°F to 73°F). It's an ideal time for hiking, exploring the charming towns, and indulging in outdoor activities.

Autumn in Menorca brings mild temperatures ranging from 18°C to 25°C (64°F to 77°F), and the island is less crowded compared to the summer months. It's a great time to enjoy the beaches, go snorkeling or diving, and immerse yourself in the local culture.

Duration of Stay

The ideal duration of your stay in Menorca depends on your interests and the activities you wish to engage in. To fully explore the island's attractions, we recommend planning a trip of at least 5 to 7 days. This will allow you to discover the main towns, relax on the beautiful beaches, and take part in various outdoor activities.

If you have limited time, a 3 to 4-day itinerary can still provide a taste of Menorca's highlights. Focus on visiting the main towns of Mahon and Ciutadella, explore a few key beaches, and indulge in the island's culinary delights.

Entry Requirements

Before traveling to Menorca, ensure you have the necessary entry requirements. If you are a citizen of the European Union or Schengen Area, you can enter Menorca with a valid national ID card or passport. Non-EU citizens should check the visa requirements for Spain and ensure they have the appropriate documents.

It's also important to have travel insurance that covers medical expenses and trip cancellations. Keep a digital and physical copy of important documents, such as your passport and insurance information, in case of emergencies.

Getting to Menorca

Menorca has its own international airport, Mahon Airport (MAH), which offers direct flights from major European cities. If you are traveling from further away, you may need to connect through a larger airport such as Barcelona or Madrid before reaching Menorca.

Alternatively, you can reach Menorca by ferry from mainland Spain. Several ferry companies operate routes between Barcelona, Valencia, and Menorca, providing a scenic and enjoyable journey.

Getting Around Menorca

Once you arrive in Menorca, you have several options for getting around the island. Renting a car is a popular choice as it provides flexibility and convenience, allowing you to explore Menorca at your own pace. The island has a well-maintained road network, making it easy to navigate between towns and attractions.

Public transportation is another option, with regular bus services connecting major towns and villages. The bus network is reliable, affordable, and offers an opportunity to interact with the local community.

For a more active and eco-friendly experience, consider renting a bicycle. Menorca has a network of cycling paths that allow you to discover the island's natural beauty while staying fit.

Accommodation Options

Menorca offers a range of accommodation options to suit different budgets and preferences. The island has luxurious resorts, boutique hotels, cozy guesthouses, and self-catering apartments. The main towns of Mahon and Ciutadella have a wide selection of accommodations, while smaller villages often have charming rural hotels or traditional farmhouses.

If you prefer a more immersive experience, you can also consider staying in a rural agrotourism establishment, where you can enjoy Menorca's countryside and engage in agricultural activities.

Packing Essentials

When packing for your trip to Menorca, it's important to consider the island's climate and the activities you plan to engage in. Here are some essential items to include in your suitcase:

- Lightweight and breathable clothing for warm weather.

- Swimwear and beach towels for enjoying the beautiful beaches.
- Comfortable walking shoes or sandals for exploring towns and natural sites.
- Sun protection essentials, including sunscreen, sunglasses, and a hat.
- A light jacket or sweater for cooler evenings.
- A reusable water bottle to stay hydrated.
- Any necessary medications or personal care items.

Remember to pack responsibly and respect the environment by avoiding single-use plastics and reducing waste during your stay.

By considering these planning aspects, you'll be well-prepared to embark on your Menorca adventure. In the following chapters, we will delve into the captivating attractions, delicious cuisine, and unique experiences that await you on this enchanting Mediterranean island.

CHAPTER 3

EXPLORING MENORCA

Menorca, a hidden gem in the Balearic Islands, offers visitors a rich tapestry of natural beauty, historical sites, and vibrant local culture. In this chapter, we will delve into the various facets of this captivating island, from its charming towns and villages to its breathtaking beaches and coves. Get ready to immerse yourself in the wonders of Menorca.

Mahon

The capital city of Menorca, Mahon, beckons travelers with its captivating blend of history and modernity. As you wander through its narrow streets, you'll encounter a treasure trove of historical sites, such as the impressive Mahon Cathedral and the fascinating archaeological site of Talatí de Dalt. History buffs will also appreciate the Museum of Menorca, which offers a deeper understanding of the island's past.

Beyond its historical allure, Mahon boasts a vibrant cultural scene. Explore the lively Mercat des Claustre, a bustling market where you can sample local delicacies and purchase fresh produce.

For an evening of entertainment, head to one of the city's charming theaters or enjoy the bustling nightlife along the harbor, where you can find a variety of bars and restaurants offering delicious Mediterranean cuisine.

Ciutadella

On the western side of Menorca lies the picturesque town of Ciutadella. Known for its enchanting medieval charm, Ciutadella captivates visitors with its narrow, winding streets, grand palaces, and beautiful churches. Explore the majestic Cathedral of Ciutadella, a stunning architectural masterpiece that dominates the town's skyline. Don't miss the historic Plaça des Born, a vibrant square lined with cafés and shops, perfect for people-watching and soaking up the lively atmosphere.

Ciutadella also offers a glimpse into Menorca's cultural heritage. Visit the Museu de Menorca in the former convent of Sant Francesc, which houses an impressive collection of archaeological artifacts, art, and historical exhibits. Immerse yourself in the local traditions by attending one of the town's colorful festivals, such as the Fiesta de Sant Joan, a lively celebration that takes place every June, featuring traditional horse parades and fireworks.

Other Towns and Villages

Beyond Mahon and Ciutadella, Menorca is dotted with charming towns and villages that are worth exploring. Alaior, situated in the center of the island, showcases a delightful mix of Moorish and Mediterranean architecture. Visit its lively town square and savor the local pastries, known as ensaimadas, in one of the traditional bakeries.

Binibeca, on the southern coast, charms visitors with its whitewashed houses and narrow streets reminiscent of a traditional fishing village. Take a leisurely stroll along its picturesque waterfront and discover hidden coves perfect for a tranquil escape.

Es Castell, located on the eastern side of Menorca, offers a more relaxed ambiance. Explore its quaint harbor, enjoy waterfront dining, and soak up the laid-back Mediterranean atmosphere.

Beaches and Coves

Menorca is renowned for its pristine beaches and secluded coves, attracting sun-seekers and nature enthusiasts alike. Cala Macarella and Cala Macarelleta, located on the southwestern coast, are picture-perfect paradises with crystal-clear turquoise waters and fine white sand.

These beaches can get crowded during peak season, so arriving early is recommended.

For a more secluded beach experience, head to Cala Pregonda on the northern coast. Accessible only by foot, this hidden gem rewards visitors with its untouched beauty and dramatic cliffs.

Families with children will enjoy Son Bou, the island's longest beach, which offers shallow waters and a range of facilities and activities for all ages.

Natural Parks and Reserves

Menorca boasts an array of natural parks and reserves, providing nature lovers with ample opportunities for exploration. The Parc Natural de s'Albufera d'Es Grau, located near Mahon, is a haven for birdwatchers, as it is home to numerous bird species and diverse ecosystems. Take a leisurely hike or rent a kayak to fully immerse yourself in this natural paradise.

The S'Arxipèlag de Cabrera National Park, located off the southern coast of Menorca, offers a unique experience for adventure enthusiasts. Explore its pristine beaches, go snorkeling in its crystal-clear waters, or take a boat tour to discover the park's rich marine life.

Outdoor Activities

Menorca's natural landscapes provide an ideal setting for outdoor activities. Embark on the Camí de Cavalls, an ancient coastal path that encircles the entire island, offering breathtaking views and opportunities for hiking, cycling, or horseback riding.

Adventurous travelers can explore the island's caves, such as the Cova d'en Xoroi, a fascinating natural cave turned into a bar and nightclub, perched on a cliff overlooking the sea. Explore the stalactite formations of the Cova des Coloms or take a boat tour to discover the mesmerizing underground lake of the Cova des Pont.

Water Sports and Diving

Menorca's crystal-clear waters make it a haven for water sports enthusiasts. Engage in activities such as snorkeling, paddleboarding, or kayaking to discover the vibrant marine life and hidden coves along the coast.

Diving enthusiasts will be captivated by the underwater wonders of Menorca. The island offers numerous diving sites, including fascinating underwater caves, shipwrecks, and stunning reefs teeming with colorful fish and marine flora.

Menorca offers a wealth of experiences for travelers seeking a blend of natural beauty, history, and culture. From the historical charm of Mahon and Ciutadella to the breathtaking beaches and coves, the island's allure is undeniable. Whether you're exploring its towns and villages, immersing yourself in nature, or indulging in water sports and diving, Menorca promises an unforgettable journey filled with discoveries and cherished memories.

CHAPTER 4

MENORCA'S CUISINE

Menorca's cuisine is a delightful reflection of its rich history and Mediterranean influences. The island's traditional dishes, local ingredients, and unique specialties offer a gastronomic experience that is sure to tantalize your taste buds. In this chapter, we will explore the diverse flavors and culinary delights that Menorca has to offer.

Traditional Dishes

Menorcan cuisine is known for its simplicity and emphasis on fresh, high-quality ingredients. One of the most famous traditional dishes is "Caldereta de Langosta," a lobster stew that showcases the island's abundant seafood. Prepared with local lobster, tomatoes, onions, and a blend of aromatic herbs and spices, this dish is a true delight for seafood lovers.

Another iconic Menorcan dish is "Sobrasada," a cured sausage made from ground pork, paprika, and various spices. It has a rich, smoky flavor and is often spread on bread or used as a filling for pastries. "Carnixulla," a dried and cured pork sausage, is another favorite among locals and visitors alike.

Local Ingredients and Specialties

Menorca's cuisine relies heavily on fresh and locally sourced ingredients. The island's fertile soil produces an abundance of vegetables, fruits, and aromatic herbs. One such ingredient is "Flor de Sal," a high-quality sea salt harvested from the island's salt flats. It is used to enhance the flavors of various dishes and is a staple in Menorcan kitchens.

Menorca is also famous for its "Queso Mahón-Menorca," a delicious cheese with a Protected Designation of Origin (PDO) status. Made from cow's milk, this cheese comes in different varieties, including young, semi-cured, and cured. It has a distinct flavor and is often enjoyed on its own or incorporated into local dishes.

Popular Restaurants and Cafés

When it comes to dining out in Menorca, you'll find a wide range of options to suit every palate and budget. The island is home to numerous restaurants and cafés that offer both traditional Menorcan cuisine and international fare. Whether you're looking for a fine dining experience or a cozy café to savor a cup of coffee, Menorca has something for everyone.

In Mahon, the capital city, you'll find a plethora of restaurants serving fresh seafood dishes, tapas, and Menorcan specialties.

The waterfront promenade is a popular spot for dining, offering picturesque views as you indulge in local delicacies.

Ciutadella, on the other hand, is known for its charming squares and narrow streets lined with restaurants. Here, you can savor traditional Menorcan cuisine in a relaxed and authentic atmosphere.

Beyond the cities, Menorca's smaller towns and villages also have hidden culinary gems. These local establishments often offer a more traditional and intimate dining experience, allowing you to immerse yourself in the island's culture and flavors.

Menorca's cuisine is a delectable fusion of fresh ingredients, traditional recipes, and Mediterranean influences. From succulent seafood dishes to cured sausages and flavorful cheeses, the island's culinary offerings are sure to captivate your senses. Whether you choose to dine in a bustling city restaurant or a quaint village eatery, Menorca's gastronomy will leave a lasting impression on your palate and create unforgettable memories of your visit to this beautiful Mediterranean island.

CHAPTER 5

MENORCA'S FESTIVALS AND EVENTS

Menorca is not only known for its stunning landscapes and pristine beaches but also for its vibrant festivals and events that showcase the island's rich cultural heritage. Throughout the year, locals and visitors alike come together to celebrate and partake in various festivities that highlight Menorca's traditions, music, and lively spirit. This chapter will provide an insight into some of the most popular festivals and events that take place on the island.

Sant Joan Festival

One of the most anticipated and iconic events in Menorca is the Sant Joan Festival, celebrated annually on June 23rd and 24th. This lively fiesta marks the beginning of summer and honors Saint John the Baptist. The festivities kick off on the eve of June 23rd with a series of bonfires known as "Nit de Sant Joan." Locals and tourists gather around the bonfires on the beaches and in the towns, enjoying music, dancing, and traditional Menorcan food.

As midnight approaches, the atmosphere becomes electrifying as the main event of the festival, the "Jaleo," takes place.

Riders on horseback known as "Caixers" gallop through the narrow streets of Ciutadella and other towns, displaying impressive horsemanship skills. The Caixers are dressed in traditional Menorcan attire, and the horses' manes and tails are adorned with colorful ribbons and flowers.

The highlight of the Jaleo is when the Caixers and their horses enter the main square, known as the "Plaza del Born," where they perform intricate choreographies while the crowd cheers and applauds. It is a spectacle that captures the essence of Menorcan culture and traditions. The Jaleo continues late into the night, accompanied by live music, dancing, and joyful celebrations.

Fiestas de Sant Antoni

Another prominent festival in Menorca is the Fiestas de Sant Antoni, celebrated in the town of Es Mercadal during the third weekend of January. This event pays homage to Saint Anthony, the patron saint of animals, and is known for its unique tradition of the "Caragol des Born," which translates to "Snail in the Square."

The festivities begin with a procession of horse-drawn carriages through the streets of Es Mercadal, accompanied by traditional music and dancing.

The highlight of the festival is the Caragol des Born, where local residents gather in the main square with their pet dogs, cats, and other animals. The animals are blessed by the parish priest, ensuring their well-being for the coming year.

Following the blessing, a series of challenging obstacles are set up in the square, forming a snail-shaped course. The participants, holding their leashed animals, navigate through the course, symbolizing the triumph over difficulties and obstacles. The Caragol des Born is a joyful and lighthearted event that brings the community together, showcasing their love and respect for animals.

Other Cultural and Music Events

Apart from the Sant Joan Festival and Fiestas de Sant Antoni, Menorca hosts a variety of other cultural and music events throughout the year. The island's capital, Mahon, is a hub for cultural activities, offering art exhibitions, concerts, and theater performances.

Music enthusiasts will find the Menorca Jazz Festival, held annually in July, a delight. This event attracts renowned jazz musicians from around the world, who perform in stunning venues, including historic courtyards and squares.

The festival creates a vibrant atmosphere, where jazz enthusiasts can immerse themselves in the captivating sounds of this genre.

For those interested in classical music, the Festival de Música de Cámara de Menorca presents a series of chamber music concerts, featuring talented musicians and ensembles. The performances take place in picturesque venues, such as ancient churches and historic manor houses, providing an intimate and enchanting setting for the audience.

Additionally, Menorca embraces its traditional music heritage with events like the Festes de Gràcia, where local folk groups perform traditional Menorcan songs and dances. These festivities offer a glimpse into the island's cultural roots and provide a unique experience for visitors to appreciate Menorca's authentic music and dance traditions.

Menorca's festivals and events offer a wonderful opportunity to immerse yourself in the island's vibrant culture, witness traditional customs, and engage in joyous celebrations. Whether you visit during the Sant Joan Festival, Fiestas de Sant Antoni, or any other cultural event, you will be captivated by the energy and passion that Menorca exudes during these special occasions.

CHAPTER 6

DAY TRIPS AND EXCURSIONS

As you explore the picturesque island of Menorca, you'll discover that there are plenty of exciting day trips and excursions to embark on beyond the main towns and beaches. These adventures will take you to hidden gems and provide you with a deeper understanding of the island's rich history, natural beauty, and cultural heritage. In this chapter, we will delve into some of the most rewarding day trips and excursions that Menorca has to offer.

Isla del Rey

One captivating day trip option is a visit to Isla del Rey, also known as King's Island. Located in the stunning natural harbor of Mahon, this small island holds significant historical importance. It was once home to a military hospital built by the British in the 18th century. Today, the island offers a fascinating glimpse into Menorca's past.

You can take a short boat ride from Mahon to Isla del Rey and explore the well-preserved ruins of the hospital complex. Wander through the atmospheric halls, courtyards, and gardens, imagining the lives of the patients and medical staff who once resided here. Don't miss the chance to visit the small museum on the island, which provides further insight into the hospital's history.

Cami de Cavalls

For nature lovers and adventure seekers, the Cami de Cavalls is an absolute must. This ancient coastal path encircles the entire island, stretching for approximately 185 kilometers. Originally used for defense purposes, it now offers hikers and cyclists an incredible opportunity to explore Menorca's diverse landscapes, from rugged cliffs to pristine beaches and lush forests.

You can choose to tackle a portion of the Cami de Cavalls that suits your interests and fitness level. Along the way, you'll encounter breathtaking vistas, hidden coves, and charming fishing villages. Be sure to pack plenty of water, snacks, and sunscreen, as the path can be challenging, especially during the hotter months. Remember to respect the natural environment and adhere to any designated rules or restrictions in protected areas.

Boat Trips to Other Islands

Menorca's strategic location in the Mediterranean Sea means that it's surrounded by other enchanting islands, each with its own unique character. Consider taking a boat trip to one of these neighboring islands for a truly memorable excursion.

One popular destination is the island of Mallorca, located to the southwest of Menorca. Mallorca boasts stunning beaches, rugged mountains, and vibrant cities like Palma de Mallorca. Explore the historic old town, visit impressive cathedrals, or simply relax on one of its famous beaches.

Another enticing option is a trip to the island of Cabrera, a pristine national park situated south of Menorca. With its crystal-clear waters and untouched landscapes, Cabrera is a paradise for snorkelers and nature enthusiasts. Explore its diverse marine life, hike along the island's trails, or simply unwind on the secluded beaches.

Nature Reserves and Rural Landscapes

Menorca is blessed with several nature reserves and rural landscapes that are worth exploring. One such reserve is the S'Albufera d'es Grau Natural Park, located in the northeast part of the island.

This protected area is a haven for birdwatchers, as it provides a sanctuary for a wide variety of migratory and resident bird species. Walk along its trails, observe the vibrant birdlife, and take in the serene beauty of the wetlands.

Additionally, the center of the island is adorned with rolling hills, lush meadows, and traditional farming villages. Rent a car or join a guided tour to discover the rural charms of Menorca. Visit idyllic farms, sample local produce, and immerse yourself in the island's agricultural heritage. Don't forget to snap some photos of the iconic Menorcan dry-stone walls that crisscross the countryside.

As you plan your day trips and excursions in Menorca, be sure to check the availability and schedules of boat trips, guided tours, and transportation options. Consider your interests and preferences, whether it's history, nature, or relaxation, and choose the experiences that resonate with you the most. These adventures beyond the main tourist areas will undoubtedly provide you with a deeper appreciation for the enchanting island of Menorca.

CHAPTER 7

PRACTICAL INFORMATION

In this chapter, we will provide you with essential practical information to ensure a smooth and enjoyable trip to Menorca. From health and safety tips to money and currency exchange, communication and internet access, local customs and etiquette, and useful phrases, we've got you covered. Let's dive in!

Health and Safety Tips

When traveling to Menorca, it's important to prioritize your health and safety. Here are some tips to keep in mind:

- Medical Facilities: Menorca has well-equipped medical facilities and hospitals that provide quality healthcare services. Familiarize yourself with the location of the nearest hospital or medical center in case of emergencies.

- Travel Insurance: It is highly recommended to have travel insurance that covers medical expenses, trip cancellation, and lost belongings. Ensure that your insurance policy includes activities such as water sports or hiking, if you plan to engage in them.

- Sun Protection: Menorca enjoys a sunny Mediterranean climate, so protect yourself from the sun's harmful rays. Use sunscreen with a high SPF, wear a hat, sunglasses, and lightweight clothing that covers your skin.

- Hydration: Stay hydrated, especially during the hot summer months. Carry a refillable water bottle and drink plenty of fluids, even if you don't feel thirsty.

- Mosquito Protection: While Menorca doesn't have a significant mosquito problem, it's advisable to take precautions, particularly during dawn and dusk. Apply insect repellent and consider wearing long sleeves and pants in areas with dense vegetation.

Money and Currency Exchange

The official currency of Menorca is the Euro (€). Here are some important points to know about money and currency exchange:

- Currency Exchange: You can exchange your currency to Euros at banks, exchange offices, and some hotels. ATMs are widely available throughout the island, allowing you to withdraw cash in Euros.

- Credit Cards: Major credit cards are widely accepted in most establishments, including hotels, restaurants, and shops. However, it's always a good idea to carry some cash for smaller vendors or places that may not accept cards.

- Tipping: Tipping is not mandatory in Menorca, but it's appreciated for good service. If you wish to leave a tip, round up the bill or add a 5-10% gratuity.

Communication and Internet

Access Staying connected while in Menorca is essential for many travelers. Here's what you need to know:

- Mobile Networks: Menorca has reliable mobile network coverage, including 4G/LTE, provided by major operators. Check with your service provider about international roaming plans and charges to ensure seamless connectivity.

- Wi-Fi Availability: Most hotels, cafes, and restaurants offer free Wi-Fi access to their customers. Additionally, there are public Wi-Fi hotspots available in popular tourist areas.

- Local SIM Cards: If you prefer to have a local number and data plan, you can purchase a prepaid SIM card from local providers. Ensure that your device is unlocked and compatible with the local network frequencies.

Local Customs and Etiquette

Respecting local customs and etiquette is important when visiting Menorca. Here are a few tips:

- Greetings: When meeting someone for the first time, a handshake is the most common form of greeting. Men and women often exchange kisses on the cheek among friends and family.

- Siesta: Menorca observes the tradition of siesta, where businesses may close for a few hours in the afternoon. Plan your activities and shopping accordingly.

- Dress Code: Menorca is generally casual, but it's advisable to dress modestly when visiting churches, religious sites, or more formal establishments.

- Respect for Nature: Menorca is known for its natural beauty, and it's essential to respect the environment.

Dispose of trash properly, stay on designated paths, and avoid damaging flora or fauna.

Language and Useful Phrases

The official language of Menorca is Catalan, but Spanish is also widely spoken. Here are some useful phrases to help you communicate:

- Hello: Hola
- Thank you: Gràcies
- Yes: Sí
- No: No
- Please: Si us plau
- Excuse me: Perdoni
- Do you speak English?: Parla anglès?
- I don't understand: No entenc
- Where is...?: On és...?
- Can you help me?: Em pot ajudar?

This chapter has provided you with important practical information to ensure a smooth and enjoyable trip to Menorca. By prioritizing your health and safety, understanding the local currency and communication options, respecting local customs and etiquette, and learning a few useful phrases, you'll be well-prepared for your adventure on this beautiful Mediterranean island. Now, let's continue exploring all that Menorca has to offer in the following chapters!

CHAPTER 8

MENORCA WITH KIDS

Traveling with kids can be an exciting and rewarding experience, and Menorca offers plenty of family-friendly activities and attractions to make your trip unforgettable. From beautiful beaches to interactive museums, there's something for everyone in the family to enjoy. In this chapter, we will explore the best kid-friendly destinations, outdoor activities, child-friendly beaches, and practical tips for traveling with kids in Menorca.

Family-Friendly Attractions

Menorca boasts a range of attractions that are perfect for families. One such place is the Menorca Zoo, located near Es Mercadal. Here, children can get up close and personal with various animals, including monkeys, giraffes, and elephants. The zoo also offers educational shows and interactive experiences, making it a fun and educational outing for kids of all ages.

Another must-visit attraction for families is the Lloc de Menorca, an interactive museum in Mahon that showcases the island's history and culture.

Kids can participate in hands-on activities, explore the exhibits, and learn about Menorca's rich heritage through engaging displays. The museum also hosts workshops and events specifically designed for children, providing them with an immersive and educational experience.

Outdoor Activities for Kids

Menorca's natural landscapes provide ample opportunities for outdoor adventures with kids. One popular activity is hiking along the Cami de Cavalls, a coastal trail that encircles the entire island. You can choose shorter, family-friendly sections of the trail, allowing children to explore the island's rugged beauty while enjoying a leisurely walk.

For a unique experience, consider taking a horseback riding tour with your kids. Several equestrian centers across Menorca offer guided tours suitable for children, allowing them to discover the island's scenic countryside from a different perspective. Whether it's a gentle trot or a more adventurous ride, horseback riding is sure to create lasting memories for the whole family.

Child-Friendly Beaches

Menorca is renowned for its pristine beaches, and many of them are well-suited for families with children. Cala Galdana, located on the southern coast, is often hailed as one of the island's most family-friendly beaches. With its shallow and calm turquoise waters, it provides a safe environment for children to swim and play. The beach is also equipped with amenities such as lifeguards, beachside restaurants, and water sports facilities, ensuring a comfortable experience for families.

Son Bou is another excellent beach option for families. It features a long stretch of golden sand, perfect for building sandcastles and playing beach games. Additionally, the shallow waters make it ideal for young children to paddle and splash around. The beach is backed by a promenade lined with shops and restaurants, making it convenient for families to grab a snack or enjoy a meal together.

Practical Tips for Traveling with Kids

When traveling with kids, it's essential to plan ahead and make necessary preparations. Here are a few practical tips to ensure a smooth and enjoyable trip:

1. Pack appropriately: Bring essential items such as sunscreen, hats, swimwear, and comfortable shoes for the whole family. It's also a good idea to pack some snacks, water, and entertainment options to keep the kids occupied during travel.

2. Plan breaks and rest days: Exploring Menorca can be tiring for both adults and children. Make sure to schedule breaks and rest days in your itinerary to allow everyone to recharge and relax.

3. Research child-friendly amenities: Before choosing accommodations, check if they offer child-friendly amenities such as cribs, high chairs, and play areas. This will make your stay more comfortable and convenient.

4. Be flexible: Traveling with kids often involves unexpected changes and detours. Embrace flexibility and be prepared to adjust your plans accordingly. Remember that creating lasting memories and enjoying quality time with your family is the ultimate goal.

Menorca is a fantastic destination for families, with its stunning landscapes, family-friendly attractions, and child-friendly beaches. From educational museums to outdoor adventures, the island offers a wide range of activities that will keep children entertained and engaged. By following practical tips and planning ahead, you can ensure a memorable and enjoyable trip for the whole family. So pack your bags, bring your sense of adventure, and get ready to create lasting memories in the beautiful island of Menorca.

CHAPTER 9

MENORCA'S HIDDEN GEMS

Menorca is a treasure trove of hidden gems waiting to be discovered. While the island is known for its stunning beaches and picturesque towns, there are lesser-known destinations that offer a more secluded and authentic experience. In this chapter, we will unveil some of Menorca's best-kept secrets and guide you to the island's hidden gems.

Off the Beaten Path Destinations

Away from the bustling tourist hotspots, Menorca boasts several off the beaten path destinations that are worth exploring. One such place is Binimel·là, a charming village tucked away in the countryside. With its traditional whitewashed houses and tranquil atmosphere, Binimel·là offers a glimpse into the island's rural life. Take a leisurely stroll through its narrow streets, visit the local church, and soak in the serene ambiance.

Another hidden gem is the village of Es Migjorn Gran, located in the heart of the island. This quaint village exudes a sense of authenticity, with its untouched architecture and laid-back vibe. Wander around the village square, savor local delicacies at family-run restaurants, and interact with friendly locals who are always eager to share their stories.

For nature enthusiasts, the Albufera des Grau Natural Park is a must-visit. This pristine wetland area is a haven for birdwatchers and nature lovers. Explore the network of walking trails that meander through marshes, dunes, and forests, and keep an eye out for rare bird species that call this park home. The park also encompasses the beautiful beach of Cala Presili, where you can relax and enjoy the tranquility of the unspoiled surroundings.

Lesser-Known Beaches and Coves

While Menorca is renowned for its beaches, there are hidden coves and secluded shores that offer a more intimate beach experience. One such gem is Cala Pilar, located on the northern coast of the island. Accessible only by foot or boat, this hidden cove is nestled between cliffs and boasts crystal-clear turquoise waters. Spend a day basking in the sun, snorkeling in the vibrant underwater world, or simply relishing the untouched beauty of this hidden paradise.

Cala Tortuga is another beach worth seeking out. Located in the northeast, this pristine stretch of sand is surrounded by sand dunes and offers a sense of seclusion.

The shallow, turquoise waters are ideal for swimming and snorkeling, making it a perfect spot for both relaxation and underwater exploration.

For a unique beach experience, head to Cala Macarella and Cala Macarelleta. These adjacent beaches are tucked away in a picturesque bay, surrounded by cliffs covered in lush vegetation. The white sand, crystal-clear waters, and stunning rock formations make them truly enchanting. While they can get crowded during peak season, visiting early in the morning or late in the afternoon can reward you with a quieter and more serene atmosphere.

Local Secrets and Recommendations

To truly uncover Menorca's hidden gems, it's always beneficial to seek insider tips and recommendations. Engage in conversations with locals and discover their favorite spots. They might guide you to hidden viewpoints that offer breathtaking panoramas, secret swimming spots known only to the locals, or hidden caves waiting to be explored.

Exploring Menorca's hidden gems is a rewarding experience that allows you to connect with the island's authentic charm. These lesser-known destinations and secluded beaches offer a chance to escape the crowds and immerse yourself in the natural beauty and rich culture of Menorca. Remember to respect the environment and leave no trace, ensuring that these hidden gems remain treasures for future visitors to discover.

CHAPTER 10

CONCLUSION

Throughout this travel guide, we have explored the captivating island of Menorca, uncovering its rich history, stunning landscapes, and vibrant culture. As we reach the end of our journey, let us take a moment to summarize the highlights that make Menorca a truly remarkable destination.

Menorca, with its pristine beaches and crystalline turquoise waters, offers a paradise for beach lovers. From the popular resorts like Cala Galdana and Son Bou to hidden gems such as Cala Macarella and Cala Mitjana, there is a beach for every preference. The untouched beauty of these sandy shores is simply breathtaking, inviting visitors to relax, swim, and soak up the Mediterranean sun.

Beyond the beaches, Menorca's towns and cities are a treasure trove of history and culture. The capital city of Mahon boasts an impressive harbor, lined with elegant Georgian buildings and charming cafes. Its narrow streets are filled with history, showcasing architectural marvels like the Church of Santa Maria and the Teatre Principal. Meanwhile, the old town of Ciutadella exudes an old-world charm, with its medieval streets, bustling markets, and the grand Cathedral of Menorca.

Nature enthusiasts will find solace in Menorca's natural parks and reserves. The Parc Natural de s'Albufera des Grau, a UNESCO Biosphere Reserve, is a haven for birdwatchers and nature lovers, offering a glimpse into the island's diverse ecosystems. The Cami de Cavalls, a coastal path that encircles the entire island, provides a fantastic opportunity for hikers and cyclists to explore Menorca's rugged coastline, hidden coves, and panoramic viewpoints.

Menorca's cuisine is another highlight not to be missed. The island's gastronomy combines Mediterranean flavors with local ingredients, resulting in a delectable fusion of tastes. Don't forget to sample the famous Mahon cheese, made from cow's milk and aged in underground caves, or indulge in the traditional seafood dishes like caldereta de llagosta (lobster stew) and stuffed calamari. For a truly authentic culinary experience, visit the local markets where you can find fresh produce, artisanal products, and mingle with the friendly locals.

Throughout the year, Menorca comes alive with vibrant festivals and events. The Sant Joan Festival, held annually on June 23rd and 24th, is a spectacle of traditional horse parades, bonfires, and fireworks that fill the streets with excitement and joy. The Fiestas de Sant Antoni, celebrated in January, showcases Menorca's deep-rooted traditions with traditional dances, music, and the famous "dimonis" (devils) procession. These festivities offer a unique opportunity to immerse oneself in the local culture and create unforgettable memories.

As we conclude our journey through Menorca, it is important to note that this guide merely scratches the surface of all that this island has to offer. Menorca is a place of endless discoveries, with hidden gems waiting to be found around every corner. Whether you seek adventure, relaxation, cultural immersion, or simply a tranquil escape, Menorca has something for everyone.

Final Tips and Recommendations

Before bidding farewell to Menorca, here are some final tips and recommendations to enhance your travel experience:

1. Respect the natural environment: Menorca is renowned for its pristine landscapes and protected areas. As responsible travelers, let us preserve the beauty of the island by respecting nature, following designated trails, and avoiding littering.

2. Embrace the local customs: Menorcans are proud of their traditions and customs. Take the time to learn a few basic phrases in the local language, show respect

for their cultural practices, and engage with the friendly locals to gain a deeper appreciation for the island's heritage.

3. Venture off the beaten path: While the popular attractions are undoubtedly captivating, don't hesitate to explore the lesser-known corners of Menorca. Venture into the countryside, discover secluded beaches, and stumble upon charming villages to truly uncover the island's hidden treasures.

4. Be mindful of the siesta: Menorca, like many Mediterranean destinations, observes the siesta tradition. During the afternoon, many shops and establishments close for a few hours. Plan your activities accordingly and embrace the relaxed pace of life on the island.

5. Capture the moments: Menorca's beauty is truly captivating, so don't forget to bring a camera or smartphone to capture the stunning landscapes, charming architecture, and memorable experiences. The island provides countless opportunities for photography enthusiasts to showcase their skills.

6. Keep an eye on local events: Check the local event calendars and festivals happening during your visit.

Menorca's cultural events, concerts, and exhibitions can enrich your travel experience and provide a deeper understanding of the island's heritage.

7. Stay hydrated: Menorca's Mediterranean climate can be warm and sunny, especially during the summer months. Remember to drink plenty of water, wear sunscreen, and seek shade when needed to stay hydrated and protect yourself from the sun.

Menorca is a destination that promises unforgettable experiences, whether you are an avid beachgoer, history enthusiast, nature lover, or food aficionado. This guide has aimed to provide you with the necessary information to plan your trip and discover the wonders of Menorca. So, pack your bags, embrace the spirit of adventure, and prepare to create lasting memories on this enchanting Balearic island. Safe travels!

Printed in Great Britain
by Amazon